A MIDSUMMER NIGHT'S DREAM

A MIDSUMMER NIGHT'S DREAM

WILLIAM SHAKESPEARE

CONTENTS

DRAMATIS PERSONÆ

THESEUS, Duke of Athens.
EGEUS, father to Hermia.
LYSANDER, in love with Hermia.
DEMETRIUS, " " " "
PHILOSTRATE, master of the revels to Theseus
QUINCE, a carpenter.
SNUG, a joiner.
BOTTOM, a weaver.
FLUTE, a bellows-mender.
SNOUT, a tinker.
STARVELING, a tailor.
HIPPOLYTA, queen of the Amazons, betrothed
    to Theseus.
HERMIA, daughter to Egeus, in love with
    Lysander.
HELENA, in love with Demetrius.
OBERON, king of the fairies.
TITANIA, queen of the fairies.
PUCK, or Robin Goodfellow.

PEASEBLOSSOM, FAIRY.

COBWEB, "

MOTH, "

MUSTARDSEED, "

Other fairies attending their King and Queen. Attendants on Theseus and Hippolyta.

SCENE—*Athens, and a wood near it.*

ACT I

SCENE I. ATHENS. THE PALACE OF THESEUS.

(Enter Theseus, Hippolyta, Philostrate, and Attendants.)

The. Now, fair Hippolyta, our nuptial hour
Draws on apace; four happy days bring in
Another moon: but, O, methinks, how slow
This old moon wanes! she lingers my desires,
005 Like to a step-dame, or a dowager,
Long withering out a young man's revenue.
Hip. Four days will quickly steep themselves
    in night;
Four nights will quickly dream away the time;
And then the moon, like to a silver bow
010 New-bent in heaven, shall behold the night
Of our solemnities.
The. Go, Philostrate,

Stir up the Athenian youth to merriments;
Awake the pert and nimble spirit of mirth:
Turn melancholy forth to funerals;
015 The pale companion is not for our pomp.
  (Exit Philostrate.)
Hippolyta, I woo'd thee with my sword,
And won thy love, doing thee injuries;
But I will wed thee in another key,
With pomp, with triumph and with revelling.

(ENTER EGEUS, HERMIA, LYSANDER, AND DEMETRIUS.)

020 **EGE.** Happy be Theseus, our renowned
  duke!
THE. Thanks, good Egeus: what's the news
  with thee?
EGE. Full of vexation come I, with complaint
Against my child, my daughter Hermia.
Stand forth, Demetrius. My noble lord,
025 This man hath my consent to marry her.
Stand forth, Lysander: and, my gracious
  duke,
This man hath bewitch'd the bosom of my
  child:
Thou, thou, Lysander, thou hast given her
  rhymes,
And interchanged love-tokens with my child:
030 Thou hast by moonlight at her window
  sung,
With feigning voice, verses of feigning love;
And stolen the impression of her fantasy

With bracelets of thy hair, rings, gawds,
    conceits,
Knacks, trifles, nosegays, sweetmeats,
    messengers
$_{035}$ Of strong prevailment in unharden'd
    youth:
With cunning hast thou filch'd my daughter's
    heart;
Turn'd her obedience, which is due to me,
To stubborn harshness: and, my gracious
    duke,
Be it so she will not here before your Grace
$_{040}$ Consent to marry with Demetrius,
I beg the ancient privilege of Athens,
As she is mine, I may dispose of her:
Which shall be either to this gentleman
Or to her death, according to our law
$_{045}$ Immediately provided in that case.

THE. What say you, Hermia? be advised, fair
    maid:
To you your father should be as a god;
One that composed your beauties; yea,
    and one
To whom you are but as a form in wax
$_{050}$ By him imprinted and within his power
To leave the figure or disfigure it.
Demetrius is a worthy gentleman.

HER. So is Lysander.

THE. In himself he is;
But in this kind, wanting your father's voice,
$_{055}$ The other must be held the worthier.

HER. I would my father look'd but with my
    eyes.

THE. Rather your eyes must with his
    judgement look.

HER. I do entreat your Grace to pardon me.
I know not by what power I am made bold,
060 Nor how it may concern my modesty,
In such a presence here to plead my thoughts;
But I beseech your Grace that I may know
The worst that may befall me in this case,
If I refuse to wed Demetrius.

065 **THE.** Either to die the death, or to abjure
For ever the society of men.
Therefore, fair Hermia, question your desires;
Know of your youth, examine well your
    blood,
Whether, if you yield not to your father's
    choice,
070 You can endure the livery of a nun;
For aye to be in shady cloister mew'd,
To live a barren sister all your life,
Chanting faint hymns to the cold fruitless
    moon.
Thrice-blessed they that master so their
    blood,
075 To undergo such maiden pilgrimage;
But earthlier happy is the rose distill'd,
Than that which, withering on the virgin
    thorn,
Grows, lives, and dies in single blessedness.

HER. So will I grow, so live, so die, my lord,

6

080 Ere I will yield my virgin patent up
Unto his lordship, whose unwished yoke
My soul consents not to give sovereignty.
THE. Take time to pause; and, by the next
    new moon,—
The sealing-day betwixt my love and me,
085 For everlasting bond of fellowship,—
Upon that day either prepare to die
For disobedience to your father's will,
Or else to wed Demetrius, as he would;
Or on Diana's altar to protest
090 For aye austerity and single life.
DEM. Relent, sweet Hermia: and, Lysander,
    yield
Thy crazed title to my certain right.
LYS. You have her father's love, Demetrius;
Let me have Hermia's: do you marry him.
095 **EGE.** Scornful Lysander! true, he hath my
    love,
And what is mine my love shall render him.
And she is mine, and all my right of her
I do estate unto Demetrius.
LYS. I am, my lord, as well derived as he,
100 As well possess'd; my love is more than his;
My fortunes every way as fairly rank'd,
If not with vantage, as Demetrius';
And, which is more than all these boasts
    can be,
I am beloved of beauteous Hermia:
105 Why should not I then prosecute my right?
Demetrius, I'll avouch it to his head,

Made love to Nedar's daughter, Helena,
And won her soul; and she, sweet lady, dotes,
Devoutly dotes, dotes in idolatry,
110 Upon this spotted and inconstant man.
THE. I must confess that I have heard so
    much,
And with Demetrius thought to have spoke
    thereof;
But, being over-full of self-affairs,
My mind did lose it. But, Demetrius, come;
115 And come, Egeus; you shall go with me,
I have some private schooling for you both.
For you, fair Hermia, look you arm yourself
To fit your fancies to your father's will;
Or else the law of Athens yields you up,—
120 Which by no means we may extenuate,—
To death, or to a vow of single life.
Come, my Hippolyta: what cheer, my love?
Demetrius and Egeus, go along:
I must employ you in some business
125 Against our nuptial, and confer with you
Of something nearly that concerns
    yourselves.
EGE. With duty and desire we follow you.
    (Exeunt all but Lysander and Hermia.)
LYS. How now, my love! why is your cheek so
    pale?
How chance the roses there do fade so fast?
130 *Her.* Belike for want of rain, which I
    could well
Beteem them from the tempest of my eyes.

8

Lys. Ay me! for aught that I could ever read,
Could ever hear by tale or history,
The course of true love never did run
    smooth;
135 But, either it was different in blood,—
Her. O cross! too high to be enthrall'd
    to low.
Lys. Or else misgraffed in respect of years,—
Her. O spite! too old to be engaged to
    young.
Lys. Or else it stood upon the choice of
    friends,—
140 *Her.* O hell! to choose love by another's
    eyes.
Lys. Or, if there were a sympathy in choice,
War, death, or sickness did lay siege to it,
Making it momentary as a sound,
Swift as a shadow, short as any dream;
145 Brief as the lightning in the collied night,
That, in a spleen, unfolds both heaven and
    earth,
And ere a man hath power to say 'Behold!'
The jaws of darkness do devour it up:
So quick bright things come to confusion.
150 *Her.* If then true lovers have been ever
    cross'd,
It stands as an edict in destiny:
Then let us teach our trial patience,
Because it is a customary cross,
As due to love as thoughts and dreams and
    sighs,

155 Wishes and tears, poor fancy's followers.

LYS. A good persuasion: therefore, hear me,
    Hermia.

I have a widow aunt, a dowager

Of great revenue, and she hath no child:

From Athens is her house remote seven
    leagues;

160 And she respects me as her only son.

There, gentle Hermia, may I marry thee;

And to that place the sharp Athenian law

Cannot pursue us. If thou lovest me, then,

Steal forth thy father's house to-morrow
    night;

165 And in the wood, a league without the
    town,

Where I did meet thee once with Helena,

To do observance to a morn of May,

There will I stay for thee.

HER. My good Lysander!

I swear to thee, by Cupid's strongest bow,

170 By his best arrow with the golden head,

By the simplicity of Venus' doves,

By that which knitteth souls and prospers
    loves,

And by that fire which burn'd the Carthage
    queen,

When the false Troyan under sail was seen,

175 By all the vows that ever men have broke,

In number more than ever women spoke,

In that same place thou hast appointed me,

To-morrow truly will I meet with thee.

Lys. Keep promise, love. Look, here comes
Helena.

(Enter Helena.)

180 **Her.** God speed fair Helena! whither
away?

Hel. Call you me fair? that fair again unsay.
Demetrius loves your fair: O happy fair!
Your eyes are lode-stars; and your tongue's
sweet air
More tuneable than lark to shepherd's ear.
185 When wheat is green, when hawthorn
buds appear.
Sickness is catching: O, were favour so,
Yours would I catch, fair Hermia, ere I go;
My ear should catch your voice, my eye
your eye,
My tongue should catch your tongue's sweet
melody.
190 Were the world mine, Demetrius being
bated,
The rest I'd give to be to you translated.
O, teach me how you look; and with what art
You sway the motion of Demetrius' heart!
Her. I frown upon him, *yet* he loves me still.
195 *Hel.* O that your frowns would teach my
smiles such skill!
Her. I give him curses, yet he gives me love.
Hel. O that my prayers could such affection
move!

HER. The more I hate, the more he
  follows me.

HEL. The more I love, the more he
  hateth me.

200 *Her.* His folly, Helena, is no fault of mine.

HEL. None, but your beauty: would that fault
  were mine!

HER. Take comfort: he no more shall see my
  face;

Lysander and myself will fly this place.

Before the time I did Lysander see,

205 Seem'd Athens as a paradise to me:

O, then, what graces in my love do dwell,

That he hath turn'd a heaven unto a hell!

LYS. Helen, to you our minds we will unfold:

To-morrow night, when Phœbe doth behold

210 Her silver visage in the watery glass,

Decking with liquid pearl the bladed grass,

A time that lovers' flights doth still conceal,

Through Athens' gates have we devised to
  steal.

HER. And in the wood, where often you
  and I

215 Upon faint primrose-beds were wont to lie,

Emptying our bosoms of their counsel sweet,

There my Lysander and myself shall meet;

And thence from Athens turn away our eyes,

To seek new friends and stranger companies.

220 Farewell, sweet playfellow: pray thou
  for us;

And good luck grant thee thy Demetrius!

Keep word, Lysander: we must starve our
    sight
From lovers' food till morrow deep
    midnight.
LYS. I will, my Hermia. *(Exit Herm.)*
Helena, adieu:
225 As you on him, Demetrius dote on you!
    (Exit.)
HEL. How happy some o'er other some
    can be!
Through Athens I am thought as fair as she.
But what of that? Demetrius thinks not so;
He will not know what all but he do know:
230 And as he errs, doting on Hermia's eyes,
So I, admiring of his qualities:
Things base and vile, holding no quantity,
Love can transpose to form and dignity:
Love looks not with the eyes, but with the
    mind;
235 And therefore is wing'd Cupid painted
    blind:
Nor hath Love's mind of any judgement
    taste;
Wings, and no eyes, figure unheedy haste:
And therefore is Love said to be a child,
Because in choice he is so oft beguiled.
240 As waggish boys in game themselves
    forswear,
So the boy Love is perjured every where:
For ere Demetrius look'd on Hermia's eyne,
He hail'd down oaths that he was only mine;

And when this hail some heat from Hermia
    felt,
245 So he dissolved, and showers of oaths did
    melt.
I will go tell him of fair Hermia's flight:
Then to the wood will he to-morrow night
Pursue her; and for this intelligence
If I have thanks, it is a dear expense:
250 But herein mean I to enrich my pain,
To have his sight thither and back again.
    (Exit.)

SCENE II. THE SAME. QUINCE'S HOUSE.

(ENTER QUINCE, SNUG, BOTTOM, FLUTE, SNOUT, AND
STARVELING.)

QUIN. Is all our company here?
BOT. You were best to call them generally,
    man by
man, according to the scrip.
QUIN. Here is the scroll of every man's
    name, which is
005 thought fit, through all Athens, to play in
    our interlude before
fore the duke and the duchess, on his
    wedding-day at night.
BOT. First, good Peter Quince, say what the
    play treats
on; then read the names of the actors; and so
    grow to a point.

010 *Quin.* Marry, our play is, The most
lamentable comedy, and most cruel death
of Pyramus and Thisby.

BOT. A very good piece of work, I assure
you, and a merry. Now, good Peter
Quince, call forth your actors by the
scroll. Masters, spread yourselves.

015 **QUIN.** Answer as I call you. Nick Bottom,
the weaver.

BOT. Ready. Name what part I am for, and
proceed.

QUIN. You, Nick Bottom, are set down for
Pyramus.

BOT. What is Pyramus? a lover, or a tyrant?

QUIN. A lover, that kills himself most gallant
for love.

020 **BOT.** That will ask some tears in the true
performing of it: if I do it, let the
audience look to their eyes; I will move
storms, I will condole in some measure.
To the rest: yet my chief humour is for a
tyrant: I could play Ercles rarely, or a part
to tear a cat in, to make all split.

025 The raging rocks
And shivering shocks
Shall break the locks
Of prison-gates;
And Phibbus' car
030 Shall shine from far,
And make and mar
The foolish Fates.

This was lofty! Now name the rest of the
players. This is Ercles' vein, a tyrant's
vein; a lover is more condoling.

035 **QUIN.** Francis Flute, the bellows-mender.

FLU. Here, Peter Quince.

QUIN. Flute, you must take Thisby on you.

FLU. What is Thisby? a wandering knight?

QUIN. It is the lady that Pyramus must love.

040 **FLU.** Nay, faith, let not me play a woman;
I have a beard coming.

QUIN. That's all one: you shall play it in a
mask, and you may speak as small as you
will.

BOT. An I may hide my face, let me play
Thisby too, I'll 045 speak in a monstrous
little voice, 'Thisne, Thisne;' 'Ah Pyramus,
my lover dear! thy Thisby dear, and lady
dear!'

QUIN. No, no; you must play Pyramus: and,
Flute, you Thisby.

BOT. Well, proceed.

050 **QUIN.** Robin Starveling, the tailor.

STAR. Here, Peter Quince.

QUIN. Robin Starveling, you must play
Thisby's mother. Tom Snout, the tinker.

SNOUT. Here, Peter Quince.

055 **QUIN.** You, Pyramus' father: myself,
Thisby's father: Snug, the joiner; you, the
lion's part: and, I hope, here is a play
fitted.

SNUG. Have you the lion's part written? pray

you, if it be, give it me, for I am slow of
study.

060 **QUIN.** You may do it extempore, for it is
nothing but roaring.

BOT. Let me play the lion too: I will roar, that
I will do any man's heart good to hear
me; I will roar, that I will make the duke
say, 'Let him roar again, let him roar 065
again.'

QUIN. An you should do it too terribly, you
would fright the duchess and the ladies,
that they would shriek; and that were
enough to hang us all.

ALL. That would hang us, every mother's
son.

070 **BOT.** I grant you, friends, if that you
should fright the ladies out of their wits,
they would have no more discretion but to
hang us: but I will aggravate my voice so,
that I will roar you as gently as any
sucking dove; I will roar you an 'twere any
nightingale.

075 **QUIN.** You can play no part but Pyramus;
for Pyramus is a sweet-faced man; a
proper man, as one shall see in a
summer's day; a most lovely, gentleman-
like man: therefore you must needs play
Pyramus.

BOT. Well, I will undertake it. What beard
were I 080 best to play it in?

QUIN. Why, what you will.

BOT. I will discharge it in either your straw
colour beard, your orange-tawny beard,
your purple-in-grain beard, or your
French crown colour beard, your perfect
085 yellow.

QUIN. Some of your French crowns have no
hair at all, and then you will play
barefaced. But, masters, here are your
parts: and I am to entreat you, request
you, and desire you, to con them by to-
morrow night; and meet me 090 in the
palace wood, a mile without the town, by
moonlight; there will we rehearse, for if
we meet in the city, we shall be dogged
with company, and our devices known. In
the meantime I will draw a bill of
properties, such as our play wants. I pray
you, fail me not.

095 **BOT.** We will meet; and there we may
rehearse most obscenely and
courageously. Take pains; be perfect:
adieu.

QUIN. At the duke's oak we meet.

BOT. Enough; hold or cut bow-strings.
(Exeunt.)

ACT II

SCENE I. A WOOD NEAR ATHENS.

(Enter, from opposite sides, a Fairy, and Puck.)

Puck. How now, spirit! whither wander you?
Fai.
Over hill, over dale,
Thorough bush, thorough brier,
Over park, over pale,
005 Thorough flood, thorough fire,
I do wander every where,
Swifter than the moon's sphere;
And I serve the fairy queen,
To dew her orbs upon the green.
010 The cowslips tall her pensioners be:
In their gold coats spots you see;
Those be rubies, fairy favours,
In those freckles live their savours:
I must go seek some dewdrops here,

$_{015}$ And hang a pearl in every cowslip's ear.
Farewell, thou lob of spirits; I'll be gone:
Our queen and all her elves come here anon.
PUCK. The king doth keep his revels here to-
    night:
Take heed the queen come not within his
    sight;
$_{020}$ For Oberon is passing fell and wrath,
Because that she as her attendant hath
A lovely boy, stolen from an Indian king;
She never had so sweet a changeling:
And jealous Oberon would have the child
$_{025}$ Knight of his train, to trace the forests
    wild;
But she perforce withholds the loved boy,
Crowns him with flowers, and makes him all
    her joy:
And now they never meet in grove or green,
By fountain clear, or spangled starlight
    sheen,
$_{030}$ But they do square, that all their elves
    for fear
Creep into acorn-cups and hide them there.
FAI. Either I mistake your shape and making
    quite,
Or else you are that shrewd and knavish
    sprite
Call'd Robin Goodfellow: are not you he
$_{035}$ That frights the maidens of the villagery;
Skim milk, and sometimes labour in the
    quern,

And bootless make the breathless housewife
    churn;
And sometime make the drink to bear no
    barm;
Mislead night-wanderers, laughing at their
    harm?
040 Those that Hobgoblin call you, and sweet
    Puck,
You do their work, and they shall have good
    luck:
Are not you he?

PUCK.

Thou speak'st aright;
I am that merry wanderer of the night.
I jest to Oberon, and make him smile,
045 When I a fat and bean-fed horse beguile,
Neighing in likeness of a filly foal:
And sometime lurk I in a gossip's bowl,
In very likeness of a roasted crab;
And when she drinks, against her lips I bob
050 And on her wither'd dewlap pour the ale.
The wisest aunt, telling the saddest tale,
Sometime for three-foot stool mistaketh me;
Then slip I from her bum, down topples she,
And 'tailor' cries, and falls into a cough;
055 And then the whole quire hold their hips
    and laugh;
And waxen in their mirth, and neeze, and
    swear
A merrier hour was never wasted there.
But, room, fairy! here comes Oberon.

Fai. And here my mistress. Would that he
were gone!

*(Enter, from one side, OBERON, with his train; from the other,
TITANIA, with hers.)*

060 ***Obe.*** Ill met by moonlight, proud Titania.
Tita. What, jealous Oberon! Fairies, skip
hence:
I have forsworn his bed and company.
Obe. Tarry, rash wanton: am not I thy lord?
Tita. Then I must be thy lady: but I know
065 When thou hast stolen away from fairy
land,
And in the shape of Corin sat all day,
Playing on pipes of corn, and versing love
To amorous Phillida. Why art thou here,
Come from the farthest steppe of India?
070 But that, forsooth, the bouncing Amazon,
Your buskin'd mistress and your warrior love,
To Theseus must be wedded, and you come
To give their bed joy and prosperity.
Obe. How canst thou thus for shame,
Titania,
075 Glance at my credit with Hippolyta,
Knowing I know thy love to Theseus?
Didst thou not lead him through the
glimmering night
From Perigenia, whom he ravished?
And make him with fair Ægle break his faith,
080 With Ariadne and Antiopa?

TITA. These are the forgeries of jealousy:
And never, since the middle summer's spring,
Met we on hill, in dale, forest, or mead,
By paved fountain or by rushy brook,
085 Or in the beached margent of the sea,
To dance our ringlets to the whistling wind,
But with thy brawls thou hast disturb'd our
    sport.
Therefore the winds, piping to us in vain,
As in revenge, have suck'd up from the sea
090 Contagious fogs; which falling in the land,
Have every pelting river made so proud,
That they have overborne their continents:
The ox hath therefore stretch'd his yoke in
    vain,
The ploughman lost his sweat; and the
    green corn
095 Hath rotted ere his youth attain'd a beard:
The fold stands empty in the drowned field,
And crows are fatted with the murrion flock;
The nine men's morris is fill'd up with mud;
And the quaint mazes in the wanton green,
100 For lack of tread, are undistinguishable:
The human mortals want their winter here;
No night is now with hymn or carol blest:
Therefore the moon, the governess of floods,
Pale in her anger, washes all the air,
105 That rheumatic diseases do abound:
And thorough this distemperature we see
The seasons alter: hoary-headed frosts
Fall in the fresh lap of the crimson rose;

And on old Hiems' thin and icy crown
₁₁₀ An odorous chaplet of sweet summer buds
Is, as in mockery, set: the spring, the summer,
The childing autumn, angry winter, change
Their wonted liveries; and the mazed world,
By their increase, now knows not which is
    which:
₁₁₅ And this same progeny of evils comes
From our debate, from our dissension;
We are their parents and original.
OBE. Do you amend it, then; it lies in you:
Why should Titania cross her Oberon?
₁₂₀ I do but beg a little changeling boy,
To be my henchman.
TITA.
Set your heart at rest:
The fairy land buys not the child of me.
His mother was a votaress of my order:
And, in the spiced Indian air, by night,
₁₂₅ Full often hath she gossip'd by my side;
And sat with me on Neptune's yellow sands,
Marking the embarked traders on the flood;
When we have laugh'd to see the sails
    conceive
And grow big-bellied with the wanton wind;
₁₃₀ Which she, with pretty and with swimming
    gait
Following,—her womb then rich with my
    young squire,—
Would imitate, and sail upon the land,
To fetch me trifles, and return again,

As from a voyage, rich with merchandise.
135 But she, being mortal, of that boy did die;
And for her sake do I rear up her boy;
And for her sake I will not part with him.
OBE. How long within this wood intend you
    stay?
TITA. Perchance till after Theseus' wedding-
    day.
140 If you will patiently dance in our round,
And see our moonlight revels, go with us;
If not, shun me, and I will spare your haunts.
OBE. Give me that boy, and I will go with
    thee.
TITA. Not for thy fairy kingdom. Fairies,
    away!
145 We shall chide downright, if I longer stay.
    (Exit Titania with her train.)
OBE. Well, go thy way: thou shalt not from
    this grove
Till I torment thee for this injury.
My gentle Puck, come hither. Thou
    rememberest
Since once I sat upon a promontory,
150 And heard a mermaid, on a dolphin's
    back,
Uttering such dulcet and harmonious breath,
That the rude sea grew civil at her song,
And certain stars shot madly from their
    spheres,
To hear the sea-maid's music.
PUCK. I remember.

155 **OBE.** That very time I saw, but thou
  couldst not,
Flying between the cold moon and the earth,
Cupid all arm'd: a certain aim he took
At a fair vestal throned by the west,
And loosed his love-shaft smartly from
  his bow,
160 As it should pierce a hundred thousand
  hearts:
But I might see young Cupid's fiery shaft
Quench'd in the chaste beams of the watery
  moon,
And the imperial votaress passed on,
In maiden meditation, fancy-free.
165 Yet mark'd I where the bolt of Cupid fell:
It fell upon a little western flower,
Before milk-white, now purple with love's
  wound,
And maidens call it love-in-idleness.
Fetch me that flower; the herb I shew'd thee
  once:
170 The juice of it on sleeping eye-lids laid
Will make or man or woman madly dote
Upon the next live creature that it sees.
Fetch me this herb; and be thou here again
Ere the leviathan can swim a league.
175 **PUCK.** I'll put a girdle round about the
  earth
In forty minutes. *(Exit.)*
OBE. Having once this juice,
I'll watch Titania when she is asleep,

And drop the liquor of it in her eyes.
The next thing then she waking looks upon,
180 Be it on lion, bear, or wolf, or bull,
On meddling monkey, or on busy ape,
She shall pursue it with the soul of love:
And ere I take this charm from off her sight,
As I can take it with another herb,
185 I'll make her render up her page to me.
But who comes here? I am invisible;
And I will overhear their conference.

(Enter Demetrius, Helena following him.)

Dem. I love thee not, therefore pursue
     me not.
Where is Lysander and fair Hermia?
190 The one I'll slay, the other slayeth me.
Thou told'st me they were stolen unto this
     wood;
And here am I, and wode within this wood,
Because I cannot meet my Hermia.
Hence, get thee gone, and follow me no
     more.
195 **Hel.** You draw me, you hard-hearted
     adamant;
But yet you draw not iron, for my heart
Is true as steel: leave you your power to draw,
And I shall have no power to follow you.
Dem. Do I entice you? do I speak you fair?
200 Or, rather, do I not in plainest truth
Tell you, I do not nor I cannot love you?

HEL. And even for that do I love you the
 more.
I am your spaniel; and, Demetrius,
The more you beat me, I will fawn on you:
205 Use me but as your spaniel, spurn me,
 strike me,
Neglect me, lose me; only give me leave,
Unworthy as I am, to follow you.
What worser place can I beg in your love,—
And yet a place of high respect with me,—
210 Than to be used as you use your dog?
DEM. Tempt not too much the hatred of my
 spirit;
For I am sick when I do look on thee.
HEL. And I am sick when I look not on you.
DEM. You do impeach your modesty too
 much,
215 To leave the city, and commit yourself
Into the hands of one that loves you not;
To trust the opportunity of night
And the ill counsel of a desert place
With the rich worth of your virginity.
220 **HEL.** Your virtue is my privilege: for that
It is not night when I do see your face,
Therefore I think I am not in the night;
Nor doth this wood lack worlds of company,
For you in my respect are all the world:
225 Then how can it be said I am alone,
When all the world is here to look on me?
DEM. I'll run from thee and hide me in the
 brakes,

And leave thee to the mercy of wild beasts.
HEL. The wildest hath not such a heart
    as you.
230 Run when you will, the story shall be
    changed:
Apollo flies, and Daphne holds the chase;
The dove pursues the griffin; the mild hind
Makes speed to catch the tiger; bootless
    speed,
When cowardice pursues, and valour flies.
235 **DEM.** I will not stay thy questions; let
    me go:
Or, if thou follow me, do not believe
But I shall do thee mischief in the wood.
HEL. Ay, in the temple, in the town, the field,
You do me mischief. Fie, Demetrius!
240 Your wrongs do set a scandal on my sex:
We cannot fight for love, as men may do;
We should be woo'd, and were not made to
    woo. *(Exit Dem.)*
I'll follow thee, and make a heaven of hell,
To die upon the hand I love so well. *(Exit.)*
245 **OBE.** Fare thee well, nymph: ere he do
    leave this grove,
Thou shalt fly him, and he shall seek thy love.

(Re-enter PUCK.)

Hast thou the flower there? Welcome,
    wanderer.
PUCK. Ay, there it is.

OBE. I pray thee, give it me.
I know a bank where the wild thyme blows,
250 Where oxlips and the nodding violet
    grows;
Quite over-canopied with luscious woodbine,
With sweet musk-roses, and with eglantine:
There sleeps Titania sometime of the night,
Lull'd in these flowers with dances and
    delight;
255 And there the snake throws her enamell'd
    skin,
Weed wide enough to wrap a fairy in:
And with the juice of this I'll streak her eyes,
And make her full of hateful fantasies.
Take thou some of it, and seek through this
    grove:
260 A sweet Athenian lady is in love
With a disdainful youth: anoint his eyes;
But do it when the next thing he espies
May be the lady: thou shalt know the man
By the Athenian garments he hath on.
265 Effect it with some care that he may prove
More fond on her than she upon her love:
And look thou meet me ere the first cock
    crow.
PUCK. Fear not, my lord, your servant shall
    do so. *(Exeunt.)*

SCENE II. ANOTHER PART OF THE WOOD.

(Enter TITANIA, with her train.)

TITA. Come, now a roundel and a fairy song;
Then, for the third part of a minute, hence;
Some to kill cankers in the musk-rose buds;
Some war with rere-mice for their leathern
    wings,
005 To make my small elves coats; and some
    keep back
The clamorous owl, that nightly hoots and
    wonders
At our quaint spirits. Sing me now asleep;
Then to your offices, and let me rest.

(SONG.)

FIR. FAIRY.
You spotted snakes with double tongue.
010 Thorny hedgehogs, be not seen;
Newts and blind-worms, do no wrong,
Come not near our fairy queen.
CHORUS.
Philomel, with melody
Sing in our sweet lullaby;
015 Lulla, lulla, lullaby, lulla, lulla, lullaby:
Never harm,
Nor spell, nor charm,
Come our lovely lady nigh;

31

So, good night, with lullaby.

FIR. FAIRY.

020 Weaving spiders, come not here;
Hence, you long-legg'd spinners, hence!
Beetles black, approach not near;
Worm nor snail, do no offence.

CHORUS.

Philomel, with melody, &c.

SEC. FAIRY.

025 Hence, away! now all is well:
One aloof stand sentinel. (Exeunt Fairies. Titania
    sleeps.)

(Enter OBERON, and squeezes the flower on Titania's eyelids.)

OBE. What thou seest when thou dost wake,
Do it for thy true-love take;
Love and languish for his sake:
030 Be it ounce, or cat, or bear,
Pard, or boar with bristled hair,
In thy eye that shall appear
When thou wakest, it is thy dear:
Wake when some vile thing is near. *(Exit.)*

(ENTER LYSANDER AND HERMIA.)

035 **LYS.** Fair love, you faint with wandering in
    the wood;
And to speak troth, I have forgot our way:
We'll rest us, Hermia, if you think it good,
And tarry for the comfort of the day.

HER. Be it so, Lysander: find you out a bed;
040 For I upon this bank will rest my head.
LYS. One turf shall serve as pillow for us both;
One heart, one bed, two bosoms, and one troth.
HER. Nay, good Lysander; for my sake, my dear,
Lie further off yet, do not lie so near.
045 ***LYS.*** O, take the sense, sweet, of my innocence!
Love takes the meaning in love's conference.
I mean, that my heart unto yours is knit,
So that but one heart we can make of it:
Two bosoms interchained with an oath;
050 So then two bosoms and a single troth.
Then by your side no bed-room me deny;
For lying so, Hermia, I do not lie.
HER. Lysander riddles very prettily:
Now much beshrew my manners and my pride,
055 If Hermia meant to say Lysander lied.
But, gentle friend, for love and courtesy
Lie further off; in human modesty,
Such separation as may well be said
Becomes a virtuous bachelor and a maid,
060 So far be distant; and, good night, sweet friend:
Thy love ne'er alter till thy sweet life end!
LYS. Amen, amen, to that fair prayer, say I;
And then end life when I end loyalty!

Here is my bed: sleep give thee all his rest!
065 **HER.** With half that wish the wisher's eyes
    be press'd! *(They sleep.)*

(Enter PUCK.)

PUCK. Through the forest have I gone,
But Athenian found I none,
On whose eyes I might approve
This flower's force in stirring love.
070 Night and silence.—Who is here?
Weeds of Athens he doth wear:
This is he, my master said,
Despised the Athenian maid;
And here the maiden, sleeping sound,
075 On the dank and dirty ground.
Pretty soul! she durst not lie
Near this lack-love, this kill-courtesy.
Churl, upon thy eyes I throw
All the power this charm doth owe.
080 When thou wakest, let love forbid
Sleep his seat on thy eyelid:
So awake when I am gone;
For I must now to Oberon. *(Exit.)*

(Enter DEMETRIUS and HELENA, running.)

HEL. Stay, though thou kill me, sweet
    Demetrius.
085 **DEM.** I charge thee, hence, and do not
    haunt me thus.

HEL. O, wilt thou darkling leave me? do
    not so.

DEM. Stay, on thy peril: I alone will go. *(Exit.)*

HEL. O, I am out of breath in this fond
    chase!

The more my prayer, the lesser is my grace.

090 Happy is Hermia, wheresoe'er she lies;

For she hath blessed and attractive eyes.

How came her eyes so bright? Not with salt
    tears:

If so, my eyes are oftener wash'd than hers.

No, no, I am as ugly as a bear;

095 For beasts that meet me run away for fear:

Therefore no marvel though Demetrius

Do, as a monster, fly my presence thus.

What wicked and dissembling glass of mine

Made me compare with Hermia's sphery eyne?

100 But who is here? Lysander! on the ground!

Dead? or asleep? I see no blood, no wound.

Lysander, if you live, good sir, awake.

LYS. *(Awaking)* And run through fire I will for
    thy sweet sake.

Transparent Helena! Nature shows art,

105 That through thy bosom makes me see thy
    heart.

Where is Demetrius? O, how fit a word

Is that vile name to perish on my sword!

HEL. Do not say so, Lysander; say not so.

What though he love your Hermia? Lord,
    what though?

₁₁₀ Yet Hermia still loves you: then be content.

LYS. Content with Hermia! No; I do repent
The tedious minutes I with her have spent.
Not Hermia but Helena I love:
Who will not change a raven for a dove?
₁₁₅ The will of man is by his reason sway'd;
And reason says you are the worthier maid.
Things growing are not ripe until their
    season:
So I, being young, till now ripe not to reason;
And touching now the point of human skill,
₁₂₀ Reason becomes the marshal to my will,
And leads me to your eyes; where I o'erlook
Love's stories, written in love's richest book.

HEL. Wherefore was I to this keen mockery
    born?
When at your hands did I deserve this scorn?
₁₂₅ Is't not enough, is't not enough,
    young man,
That I did never, no, nor never can,
Deserve a sweet look from Demetrius' eye,
But you must flout my insufficiency?
Good troth, you do me wrong, good sooth,
    you do,
₁₃₀ In such disdainful manner me to woo.
But fare you well: perforce I must confess
I thought you lord of more true gentleness.
O, that a lady, of one man refused,
Should of another therefore be abused! *(Exit).*

₁₃₅ **LYS.** She sees not Hermia. Hermia, sleep
    thou there:

And never mayst thou come Lysander near!
For as a surfeit of the sweetest things
The deepest loathing to the stomach brings,
Or as the heresies that men do leave
₁₄₀ Are hated most of those they did deceive,
So thou, my surfeit and my heresy,
Of all be hated, but the most of me!
And, all my powers, address your love and
    might
To honour Helen and to be her knight! *(Exit.)*
₁₄₅ **HER.** *(Awaking)* Help me, Lysander, help
    me! do thy best
To pluck this crawling serpent from my
    breast!
Ay me, for pity! what a dream was here!
Lysander, look how I do quake with fear:
Methought a serpent eat my heart away,
₁₅₀ And you sat smiling at his cruel prey.
Lysander! what, removed? Lysander! lord!
What, out of hearing? gone? no sound, no
    word?
Alack, where are you? speak, an if you hear;
Speak, of all loves! I swoon almost with fear.
₁₅₅ No? then I well perceive you are not nigh:
Either death or you I'll find immediately.
    (Exit.)

ACT III

SCENE I. THE WOOD. TITANIA LYING ASLEEP.

(ENTER QUINCE, SNUG, BOTTOM, FLUTE, SNOUT, AND STARVELING.)

Bot. Are we all met?

Quin. Pat, pat; and here's a marvellous convenient place for our rehearsal. This green plot shall be our stage, this hawthorn-brake our tiring-house; and we will do it in $_{005}$ action as we will do it before the duke.

Bot. Peter Quince,—

Quin. What sayest thou, bully Bottom?

Bot. There are things in this comedy of Pyramus and Thisby that will never please. First, Pyramus must draw $_{010}$ a

sword to kill himself; which the ladies
cannot abide. How answer you that?

SNOUT. By'r lakin, a parlous fear.

STAR. I believe we must leave the killing out,
when all is done.

015 **BOT.** Not a whit: I have a device to make
all well. Write me a prologue; and let the
prologue seem to say, we will do no harm
with our swords, and that Pyramus is not
killed indeed; and, for the more better
assurance, tell them that I Pyramus am
not Pyramus, but Bottom the weaver: 020
this will put them out of fear.

QUIN. Well, we will have such a prologue;
and it shall be written in eight and six.

BOT. No, make it two more; let it be written
in eight and eight.

025 **SNOUT.** Will not the ladies be afeard of
the lion?

STAR. I fear it, I promise you.

BOT. Masters, you ought to consider with
yourselves: to bring in,—God shield us!—
a lion among ladies, is a most dreadful
thing; for there is not a more fearful wild-
fowl 030 than your lion living; and we
ought to look to 't.

SNOUT. Therefore another prologue must tell
he is not a lion.

BOT. Nay, you must name his name, and
half his face must be seen through the
lion's neck; and he himself must 035

speak through, saying thus, or to the
same defect,—'Ladies,' —or, 'Fair ladies,
—I would wish you,'—or, 'I would
request you,'—or, 'I would entreat you,
—not to fear, not to tremble: my life for
yours. If you think I come hither as a
lion, it were pity of my life: no, I am no
such thing; I $_{040}$ am a man as other men
are:' and there indeed let him name his
name, and tell them plainly, he is Snug
the joiner.

Quin. Well, it shall be so. But there is two
hard things; that is, to bring the
moonlight into a chamber; for, you know,
Pyramus and Thisby meet by moonlight.

$_{045}$ **Snout.** Doth the moon shine that night
we play our play?

Bot. A calendar, a calendar! look in the
almanac; find out moonshine, find out
moonshine.

Quin. Yes, it doth shine that night.

Bot. Why, then may you leave a casement of
the great $_{050}$ chamber window, where we
play, open, and the moon may shine in at
the casement.

Quin. Ay; or else one must come in with a
bush of thorns and a lantern, and say he
comes to disfigure, or to present, the
person of moonshine. Then, there is
another $_{055}$ thing: we must have a wall in
the great chamber; for Pyramus and

Thisby, says the story, did talk through the
chink of a wall.

SNOUT. You can never bring in a wall. What
say you, Bottom?

060 **BOT.** Some man or other must present
wall: and let him have some plaster, or
some loam, or some rough-cast about
him, to signify wall; and let him hold his
fingers thus, and through that cranny shall
Pyramus and Thisby whisper.

QUIN. If that may be, then all is well. Come,
sit 065 down, every mother's son, and
rehearse your parts. Pyramus, you begin:
when you have spoken your speech, enter
into that brake: and so every one
according to his cue.

(Enter PUCK behind.)

PUCK. What hempen home-spuns have we
swaggering here,
So near the cradle of the fairy queen?
070 What, a play toward! I'll be an auditor;
An actor too perhaps, if I see cause.

QUIN. Speak, Pyramus. Thisby, stand forth.

BOT. Thisby, the flowers of odious savours
sweet,——

QUIN. Odours, odours.

075 **BOT.** —— odours savours sweet:
So hath thy breath, my dearest Thisby dear.
But hark, a voice! stay thou but here awhile,

42

And by and by I will to thee appear. *(Exit.)*

PUCK. A stranger Pyramus than e'er play'd
here. *(Exit.)*

080 **FLU.** Must I speak now?

QUIN. Ay, marry, must you; for you must
understand he

goes but to see a noise that he heard, and is to
come again.

FLU. Most radiant Pyramus, most lily-white
of hue,

Of colour like the red rose on triumphant
brier,

085 Most brisky juvenal, and eke most
lovely Jew,

As true as truest horse, that yet would never
tire,

I'll meet thee, Pyramus, at Ninny's tomb.

QUIN. 'Ninus' tomb,' man: why, you must not
speak that yet; that you answer to
Pyramus: you speak all your 090 part at
once, cues and all. Pyramus enter: your
cue is past; it is, 'never tire.'

FLU. O,—As true as truest horse, that yet
would never tire.

(Re-enter PUCK, and BOTTOM with an ass's head.)

BOT. If I were fair, Thisby, I were only
thine.

QUIN. O monstrous! O strange! we are
haunted. Pray, 095 masters! fly, masters!

43

Help! *(Exeunt Quince, Snug, Flute, Snout, and Starveling.)*

Puck. I'll follow you, I'll lead you about a round,

Through bog, through bush, through brake, through brier:

Sometime a horse I'll be, sometime a hound,

A hog, a headless bear, sometime a fire;

100 And neigh, and bark, and grunt, and roar, and burn,

Like horse, hound, hog, bear, fire, at every turn. *(Exit.)*

Bot. Why do they run away? this is a knavery of them to make me afeard.

(Re-enter Snout.)

Snout. O bottom, thou art changed! what do I see on 105 thee?

Bot. What do you see? you see an ass-head of your own, do you? *(Exit Snout.)*

(Re-enter Quince.)

Quin. Bless thee, Bottom! bless thee! thou art translated. *(Exit.)*

110 **Bot.** I see their knavery: this is to make an ass of me; to fright me, if they could. But I will not stir from this place, do what they can: I will walk up and down here, and I

will sing, that they shall hear I am not
    afraid. *(Sings.)*

The ousel cock so black of hue,
₁₁₅ With orange-tawny bill,
The throstle with his note so true,
The wren with little quill;

TITA. *(Awaking)* What angel wakes me from
    my flowery bed?

BOT. *(Sings)*

The finch, the sparrow, and the lark,
₁₂₀ The plain-song cuckoo gray,
Whose note full many a man doth mark,
And dares not answer nay;—

for, indeed, who would set his wit to so foolish
    a bird? who would give a bird the lie,
    though he cry 'cuckoo' never so?

₁₂₅ **TITA.** I pray thee, gentle mortal, sing
    again:
Mine ear is much enamour'd of thy note;
So is mine eye enthralled to thy shape;
And thy fair virtue's force perforce doth
    move me
On the first view to say, to swear, I love thee.

₁₃₀ **BOT.** Methinks, mistress, you should have
    little reason for that: and yet, to say the
    truth, reason and love keep little company
    together now-a-days; the more the pity,
    that some honest neighbours will not
    make them friends. Nay, I can gleek upon
    occasion.

135 **TITA.** Thou art as wise as thou art
beautiful.

BOT. Not so, neither: but if I had wit enough
to get out of this wood, I have enough to
serve mine own turn.

TITA. Out of this wood do not desire to go:
Thou shalt remain here, whether thou wilt
or no.

140 I am a spirit of no common rate:
The summer still doth tend upon my state;
And I do love thee: therefore, go with me;
I'll give thee fairies to attend on thee;
And they shall fetch thee jewels from the
deep,

145 And sing, while thou on pressed flowers
dost sleep:
And I will purge thy mortal grossness so,
That thou shalt like an airy spirit go.
Peaseblossom! Cobweb! Moth! and
Mustardseed!

*(ENTER PEASEBLOSSOM, COBWEB, MOTH, AND
MUSTARDSEED.)*

FIRST FAI. Ready.
SEC. FAI. And I.
THIRD FAI. And I.
FOURTH FAI. And I.
ALL. Where shall we go?
150 **TITA.** Be kind and courteous to this
gentleman;

Hop in his walks, and gambol in his eyes;
Feed him with apricocks and dewberries,
With purple grapes, green figs, and
    mulberries;
The honey-bags steal from the humble-bees,
155 And for night-tapers crop their waxen
    thighs,
And light them at the fiery glow-worm's eyes,
To have my love to bed and to arise;
And pluck the wings from painted butterflies
To fan the moonbeams from his sleeping eyes:
160 Nod to him, elves, and do him courtesies.

FIRST FAI. Hail, mortal!

SEC. FAI. *Hail!*

THIRD FAI. *Hail!*

FOURTH FAI. *Hail!*

165 **BOT.** I cry your worships mercy, heartily: I
beseech your worship's name.

COB. Cobweb.

BOT. I shall desire you of more
acquaintance, good Master Cobweb: if I
cut my finger, I shall make bold with 170
you. Your name, honest gentleman?

PEAS. Peaseblossom.

BOT. I pray you, commend me to Mistress
Squash, your mother, and to Master
Peascod, your father. Good Master
Peaseblossom, I shall desire you of more
acquaintance 175 too. Your name, I
beseech you, sir?

MUS. Mustardseed.

Bot. Good Master Mustardseed, I know
your patience well: that same cowardly,
giant-like ox-beef hath devoured many a
gentleman of your house: I promise you
₁₈₀ your kindred hath made my eyes water
ere now. I desire your more acquaintance,
good Master Mustardseed.

Tita. Come, wait upon him; lead him to my
bower.
The moon methinks looks with a watery eye;
And when she weeps, weeps every little
flower,
₁₈₅ Lamenting some enforced chastity.
Tie up my love's tongue, bring him silently.
(Exeunt.)

SCENE II. ANOTHER PART OF THE WOOD.

(Enter OBERON.)

Obe. I wonder if Titania be awaked;
Then, what it was that next came in her eye,
Which she must dote on in extremity.

(Enter PUCK.)

Here comes my messenger.
How now, mad spirit!
₀₀₅ What night-rule now about this haunted
grove?

PUCK. My mistress with a monster is in love.
Near to her close and consecrated bower,
While she was in her dull and sleeping hour,
A crew of patches, rude mechanicals,
010 That work for bread upon Athenian stalls,
Were met together to rehearse a play,
Intended for great Theseus' nuptial-day.
The shallowest thick-skin of that barren sort,
Who Pyramus presented, in their sport
015 Forsook his scene, and enter'd in a brake:
When I did him at this advantage take,
An ass's nole I fixed on his head:
Anon his Thisbe must be answered,
And forth my mimic comes. When they
    him spy,
020 As wild geese that the creeping fowler eye,
Or russet-pated choughs, many in sort,
Rising and cawing at the gun's report,
Sever themselves and madly sweep the sky,
So, at his sight, away his fellows fly;
025 And, at our stamp, here o'er and o'er one
    falls;
He murder cries, and help from Athens calls.
Their sense thus weak, lost with their fears
    thus strong,
Made senseless things begin to do them
    wrong;
For briers and thorns at their apparel snatch;
030 Some sleeves, some hats, from yielders all
    things catch.
I led them on in this distracted fear,

And left sweet Pyramus translated there:
When in that moment, so it came to pass,
Titania waked, and straightway loved an ass.
035 **OBE.** This falls out better than I could
    devise.
But hast thou yet latch'd the Athenian's eyes
With the love-juice, as I did bid thee do?
PUCK. I took him sleeping,—that is finish'd
    too,—
And the Athenian woman by his side;
040 That, when he waked, of force she must
    be eyed.

(ENTER HERMIA AND DEMETRIUS.)

OBE. Stand close: this is the same Athenian.
PUCK. This is the woman, but not this
    the man.
DEM. O, why rebuke you him that loves
    you so?
Lay breath so bitter on your bitter foe.
045 **HER.** Now I but chide; but I should use
    thee worse,
For thou, I fear, hast given me cause to curse.
If thou hast slain Lysander in his sleep,
Being o'er shoes in blood, plunge in the
    deep,
And kill me too.
050 The sun was not so true unto the day
As he to me: would he have stolen away
From sleeping Hermia? I'll believe as soon

This whole earth may be bored, and that
    the moon
May through the centre creep, and so
    displease
055 Her brother's noontide with the
    Antipodes.
It cannot be but thou hast murder'd him;
So should a murderer look, so dead, so grim.
DEM. So should the murder'd look; and so
    should I,
Pierced through the heart with your stern
    cruelty:
060 Yet you, the murderer, look as bright, as
    clear,
As yonder Venus in her glimmering sphere.
HER. What's this to my Lysander? where
    is he?
Ah, good Demetrius, wilt thou give him me?
DEM. I had rather give his carcass to my
    hounds.
065 **HER.** Out, dog! out, cur! thou drivest me
    past the bounds
Of maiden's patience. Hast thou slain him,
    then?
Henceforth be never number'd among men!
O, once tell true, tell true, even for my sake!
Durst thou have look'd upon him being
    awake,
070 And hast thou kill'd him sleeping? O brave
    touch!
Could not a worm, an adder, do so much?

An adder did it; for with doubler tongue
Than thine, thou serpent, never adder stung.

DEM. You spend your passion on a misprised mood:

075 I am not guilty of Lysander's blood;
Nor is he dead, for aught that I can tell.

HER. I pray thee, tell me then that he is well.

DEM. An if I could, what should I get therefore?

HER. A privilege, never to see me more.
080 And from thy hated presence part I so:
See me no more, whether he be dead or no.
(Exit.)

DEM. There is no following her in this fierce vein:
Here therefore for a while I will remain.
So sorrow's heaviness doth heavier grow
085 For debt that bankrupt sleep doth sorrow owe;
Which now in some slight measure it will pay,
If for his tender here I make some stay. *(Lies down and sleeps.)*

OBE. What hast thou done? thou hast mistaken quite,
And laid the love-juice on some true-love's sight:
090 Of thy misprision must perforce ensue
Some true love turn'd, and not a false turn'd true.

PUCK. Then fate o'er-rules, that, one man holding troth,

A million fail, confounding oath on oath.

OBE. About the wood go swifter than the
    wind,

095 And Helena of Athens look thou find:

All fancy-sick she is and pale of cheer,

With sighs of love, that costs the fresh blood
    dear:

By some illusion see thou bring her here:

I'll charm his eyes against she do appear.

100 **PUCK.** I go, I go; look how I go,

Swifter than arrow from the Tartar's bow.

    (Exit.)

OBE. Flower of this purple dye,

Hit with Cupid's archery,

Sink in apple of his eye.

105 When his love he doth espy,

Let her shine as gloriously

As the Venus of the sky.

When thou wakest, if she be by,

Beg of her for remedy.

    (Re-enter PUCK.)

PUCK. 110 Captain of our fairy band,

Helena is here at hand;

And the youth, mistook by me,

Pleading for a lover's fee.

Shall we their fond pageant see?

115 Lord, what fools these mortals be!

OBE. Stand aside: the noise they make

Will cause Demetrius to awake.

53

PUCK. Then will two at once woo one;
That must needs be sport alone;
120 And those things do best please me
That befal preposterously.

(ENTER LYSANDER AND HELENA.)

LYS. Why should you think that I should woo
    in scorn?
Scorn and derision never come in tears:
Look, when I vow, I weep; and vows so born,
125 In their nativity all truth appears.
How can these things in me seem scorn
    to you,
Bearing the badge of faith, to prove them
    true?
HEL. You do advance your cunning more
    and more.
When truth kills truth, O devilish-holy fray!
130 These vows are Hermia's: will you give her
    o'er?
Weigh oath with oath, and you will nothing
    weigh:
Your vows to her and me, put in two scales,
Will even weigh; and both as light as tales.
LYS. I had no judgement when to her I
    swore.
135 **HEL.** Nor none, in my mind, now you give
    her o'er.
LYS. Demetrius loves her, and he loves
    not you.

DEM. *(Awaking)* O Helen, goddess, nymph,
    perfect, divine!
To what, my love, shall I compare thine eyne?
Crystal is muddy. O, how ripe in show
140 Thy lips, those kissing cherries, tempting
    grow!
That pure congealed white, high Taurus'
    snow,
Fann'd with the eastern wind, turns to a crow
When thou hold'st up thy hand: O, let me kiss
This princess of pure white, this seal of bliss!
145 **HEL.** O spite! O hell! I see you all are bent
To set against me for your merriment:
If you were civil and knew courtesy,
You would not do me thus much injury.
Can you not hate me, as I know you do,
150 But you must join in souls to mock me too?
If you were men, as men you are in show,
You would not use a gentle lady so;
To vow, and swear, and superpraise my parts,
When I am sure you hate me with your
    hearts.
155 You both are rivals, and love Hermia;
And now both rivals, to mock Helena:
A trim exploit, a manly enterprise,
To conjure tears up in a poor maid's eyes
With your derision! none of noble sort
160 Would so offend a virgin, and extort
A poor soul's patience, all to make you sport.
LYS. You are unkind, Demetrius; be not so;
For you love Hermia; this you know I know:

And here, with all good will, with all my
    heart,
165 In Hermia's love I yield you up my part;
And yours of Helena to me bequeath,
Whom I do love, and will do till my death.

HEL. Never did mockers waste more idle
    breath.

DEM. Lysander, keep thy Hermia; I will
    none:
170 If e'er I loved her, all that love is gone.
My heart to her but as guest-wise sojourn'd,
And now to Helen is it home return'd,
There to remain.

LYS. Helen, it is not so.

DEM. Disparage not the faith thou dost not
    know,
175 Lest, to thy peril, thou aby it dear.
Look, where thy love comes; yonder is thy
    dear.

(Re-enter HERMIA.)

HER. Dark night, that from the eye his
    function takes,
The ear more quick of apprehension makes;
Wherein it doth impair the seeing sense,
180 It pays the hearing double recompense.
Thou art not by mine eye, Lysander, found;
Mine ear, I thank it, brought me to thy
    sound.
But why unkindly didst thou leave me so?

Lys. Why should he stay, whom love doth
    press to go?

185 **Her.** What love could press Lysander
    from my side?

Lys. Lysander's love, that would not let him
    bide,

Fair Helena, who more engilds the night

Than all yon fiery oes and eyes of light.

Why seek'st thou me? could not this make
    thee know,

190 The hate I bear thee made me leave
    thee so?

Her. You speak not as you think: it
    cannot be.

Hel. Lo, she is one of this confederacy!

Now I perceive they have conjoin'd all three

To fashion this false sport, in spite of me.

195 Injurious Hermia! most ungrateful maid!

Have you conspired, have you with these
    contrived

To bait me with this foul derision?

Is all the counsel that we two have shared,

The sisters' vows, the hours that we have
    spent,

200 When we have chid the hasty-footed time

For parting us,—O, is all forgot?

All school-days' friendship, childhood
    innocence?

We, Hermia, like two artificial gods,

Have with our needles created both one
    flower,

₂₀₅ Both on one sampler, sitting on one
    cushion,
Both warbling of one song, both in one key;
As if our hands, our sides, voices, and minds,
Had been incorporate. So we grew together,
Like to a double cherry, seeming parted;
₂₁₀ But yet an union in partition,
Two lovely berries moulded on one stem;
So, with two seeming bodies, but one heart;
Two of the first, like coats in heraldry,
Due but to one, and crowned with one crest.
₂₁₅ And will you rent our ancient love
    asunder,
To join with men in scorning your poor
    friend?
It is not friendly, 'tis not maidenly:
Our sex, as well as I, may chide you for it,
Though I alone do feel the injury.
₂₂₀ **HER.** I am amazed at your passionate
    words.
I scorn you not: it seems that you scorn me.
HEL. Have you not set Lysander, as in scorn,
To follow me and praise my eyes and face?
And made your other love, Demetrius,
₂₂₅ Who even but now did spurn me with his
    foot,
To call me goddess, nymph, divine and rare,
Precious, celestial? Wherefore speaks he this
To her he hates? and wherefore doth
    Lysander
Deny your love, so rich within his soul,

₂₃₀ And tender me, forsooth, affection,
But by your setting on, by your consent?
What though I be not so in grace as you,
So hung upon with love, so fortunate,
But miserable most, to love unloved?
₂₃₅ This you should pity rather than despise.

HER. I understand not what you mean by
this.

HEL. Ay, do, persever, counterfeit sad looks,
Make mouths upon me when I turn my back;
Wink each at other; hold the sweet jest up:
₂₄₀ This sport, well carried, shall be
chronicled.
If you have any pity, grace, or manners,
You would not make me such an argument.
But fare ye well: 'tis partly my own fault;
Which death or absence soon shall remedy.

₂₄₅ **LYS.** Stay, gentle Helena; hear my excuse:
My love, my life, my soul, fair Helena!

HEL. O excellent!

HER. Sweet, do not scorn her so.

DEM. If she cannot entreat, I can compel.

LYS. Thou canst compel no more than she
entreat:
₂₅₀ Thy threats have no more strength than
her weak prayers.
Helen, I love thee; by my life, I do:
I swear by that which I will lose for thee,
To prove him false that says I love thee not.

DEM. I say I love thee more than he can do.

₂₅₅ **LYS.** If thou say so, withdraw, and prove

it too.

DEM. Quick, come!

HER. Lysander, whereto tends all this?

LYS. Away, you Ethiope!

DEM. No, no; he'll . . .

Seem to break loose; take on as you would follow,

But yet come not: you are a tame man, go!

₂₆₀ **LYS.** Hang off, thou cat, thou burr! vile thing, let loose,

Or I will shake thee from me like a serpent!

HER. Why are you grown so rude? what change is this?

Sweet love,—

LYS. Thy love! out, tawny Tartar, out!

Out, loathed medicine! hated potion, hence!

HER. Do you not jest?

HEL.

₂₆₅ Yes, sooth; and so do you.

LYS. Demetrius, I will keep my word with thee.

DEM. I would I had your bond, for I perceive

A weak bond holds you: I'll not trust your word.

LYS. What, should I hurt her, strike her, kill her dead?

₂₇₀ Although I hate her, I'll not harm her so.

HER. What, can you do me greater harm than hate?

Hate me! wherefore? O me! what news, my love!

Am not I Hermia? are not you Lysander?
I am as fair now as I was erewhile.
₂₇₅ Since night you loved me; yet since night
    you left me:
Why, then you left me,—O, the gods forbid!
    —

In earnest, shall I say?
Lys. Ay, by my life;
And never did desire to see thee more.
Therefore be out of hope, of question, of
    doubt;
₂₈₀ Be certain, nothing truer; 'tis no jest
That I do hate thee, and love Helena.
Her. O me! you juggler! you canker-
    blossom!
You thief of love! what, have you come by
    night
And stolen my love's heart from him?
Hel. Fine, i'faith!
₂₈₅ Have you no modesty, no maiden shame,
No touch of bashfulness? What, will you tear
Impatient answers from my gentle tongue?
Fie, fie! you counterfeit, you puppet, you!
Her. Puppet? why so? ay, that way goes the
    game.
₂₉₀ Now I perceive that she hath made
    compare
Between our statures; she hath urged her
    height;
And with her personage, her tall personage,
Her height, forsooth, she hath prevail'd

with him.
And are you grown so high in his esteem,
295 Because I am so dwarfish and so low?
How low am I, thou painted maypole? speak;
How low am I? I am not yet so low
But that my nails can reach unto thine eyes.
HEL. I pray you, though you mock me, gentlemen,
300 Let her not hurt me: I was never curst;
I have no gift at all in shrewishness;
I am a right maid for my cowardice:
Let her not strike me. You perhaps may think,
Because she is something lower than myself,
That I can match her.
HER. 305 Lower! hark, again.
HEL. Good Hermia, do not be so bitter with me
I evermore did love you, Hermia,
Did ever keep your counsels, never wrong'd you;
Save that, in love unto Demetrius,
310 I told him of your stealth unto this wood.
He follow'd you; for love I follow'd him;
But he hath chid me hence, and threaten'd me
To strike me, spurn me, nay, to kill me too:
And now, so you will let me quiet go,
315 To Athens will I bear my folly back,
And follow you no further: let me go:
You see how simple and how fond I am.
HER. Why, get you gone: who is't that

hinders you?

HEL. A foolish heart, that I leave here behind.

HER. What, with Lysander?

HEL. ₃₂₀ With Demetrius.

LYS. Be not afraid; she shall not harm thee, Helena.

DEM. No, sir, she shall not, though you take her part.

HEL. O, when she's angry, she is keen and shrewd!

She was a vixen when she went to school;

₃₂₅ And though she be but little, she is fierce.

HER. Little again! nothing but low and little!

Why will you suffer her to flout me thus?

Let me come to her.

LYS. Get you gone, you dwarf;

You minimus, of hindering knot-grass made;

You bead, you acorn.

DEM. ₃₃₀ You are too officious

In her behalf that scorns your services.

Let her alone: speak not of Helena;

Take not her part; for, if thou dost intend

Never so little show of love to her,

₃₃₅ Thou shalt aby it.

LYS. Now she holds me not;

Now follow, if thou darest, to try whose right,

Of thine or mine, is most in Helena.

DEM. Follow! nay, I'll go with thee, cheek by jole. *(Exeunt Lysander and Demetrius.)*

HER. You, mistress, all this coil is 'long

of you:

Nay, go not back.

HEL. 340 I will not trust you, I,

Nor longer stay in your curst company.

Your hands than mine are quicker for a fray,

My legs are longer though, to run away.

(Exit.)

HER. I am amazed, and know not what to
   say. *(Exit.)*

345 **OBE.** This is thy negligence: still thou
   mistakest,

Or else committ'st thy knaveries wilfully.

PUCK. Believe me, king of shadows, I
   mistook.

Did not you tell me I should know the man

By the Athenian garments he had on?

350 And so far blameless proves my enterprise,

That I have 'nointed an Athenian's eyes;

And so far am I glad it so did sort,

As this their jangling I esteem a sport.

OBE. Thou see'st these lovers seek a place to
   fight:

355 Hie therefore, Robin, overcast the night;

The starry welkin cover thou anon

With drooping fog, as black as Acheron;

And lead these testy rivals so astray,

As one come not within another's way.

360 Like to Lysander sometime frame thy
   tongue,

Then stir Demetrius up with bitter wrong;

And sometime rail thou like Demetrius;

And from each other look thou lead them
    thus.
Till o'er their brows death-counterfeiting
    sleep
365 With leaden legs and batty wings doth
    creep:
Then crush this herb into Lysander's eye;
Whose liquor hath this virtuous property,
To take from thence all error with his might,
And make his eyeballs roll with wonted sight.
370 When they next wake, all this derision
Shall seem a dream and fruitless vision;
And back to Athens shall the lovers wend,
With league whose date till death shall
    never end.
Whiles I in this affair do thee employ,
375 I'll to my queen and beg her Indian boy;
And then I will her charmed eye release
From monster's view, and all things shall be
    peace.
PUCK. My fairy lord, this must be done with
    haste,
For night's swift dragons cut the clouds full
    fast,
380 And yonder shines Aurora's harbinger;
At whose approach, ghosts, wandering here
    and there,
Troop home to churchyards: damned spirits
    all,
That in crossways and floods have burial,
Already to their wormy beds are gone;

₃₈₅ For fear lest day should look their shames
  upon,
They wilfully themselves exile from light,
And must for aye consort with black-brow'd
  night.
OBE. But we are spirits of another sort:
I with the morning's love have oft made sport;
₃₉₀ And, like a forester, the groves may tread,
Even till the eastern gate, all fiery-red,
Opening on Neptune with fair blessed beams,
Turns into yellow gold his salt green streams.
But, notwithstanding, haste; make no delay:
₃₉₅ We may effect this business yet ere day.
    (Exit.)
PUCK. Up and down, up and down,
I will lead them up and down:
I am fear'd in field and town:
Goblin, lead them up and down.
₄₀₀ Here comes one.

(Re-enter LYSANDER.)

LYS. Where art thou, proud Demetrius?
  speak thou now.
PUCK. Here, villain; drawn and ready. Where
  art thou?
LYS. I will be with thee straight.
PUCK.
Follow me, then,
To plainer ground. *(Exit Lysander, as following
  the voice.)*

(RE-ENTER DEMETRIUS.)

DEM. Lysander! speak again:
405 Thou runaway, thou coward, art thou fled?
Speak! In some bush? Where dost thou hide
    thy head?
PUCK. Thou coward, art thou bragging to
    the stars,
Telling the bushes that thou look'st for wars,
And wilt not come? Come, recreant; come,
    thou child;
410 I'll whip thee with a rod: he is defiled
That draws a sword on thee.
DEM. Yea, art thou there?
PUCK. Follow my voice: we'll try no
    manhood here. *(Exeunt.)*

(Re-enter LYSANDER.)

LYS. He goes before me and still dares me on:
When I come where he calls, then he is gone.
415 The villain is much lighter-heel'd than I:
I follow'd fast, but faster he did fly;
That fallen am I in dark uneven way,
And here will rest me. *(Lies down.)* Come, thou
    gentle day!
For if but once thou show me thy grey light,
420 I'll find Demetrius, and revenge this spite.
    (Sleeps.)

(RE-ENTER PUCK AND DEMETRIUS.)

PUCK. Ho, ho, ho! Coward, why comest
    thou not?

DEM. Abide me, if thou darest; for well I wot
Thou runn'st before me, shifting every place,
And darest not stand, nor look me in the face.
425 Where art thou now?

PUCK.

425 Come hither: I am here.

DEM. Nay, then, thou mock'st me. Thou
    shalt buy this dear,

If ever I thy face by daylight see:
Now, go thy way. Faintness constraineth me
To measure out my length on this cold bed.
430 By day's approach look to be visited. *(Lies
    down and sleeps.)*

(Re-enter HELENA.)

HEL. O weary night, O long and tedious
    night,

Abate thy hours! Shine comforts from the
    east,

That I may back to Athens by daylight,
From these that my poor company detest:
435 And sleep, that sometimes shuts up
    sorrow's eye,

Steal me awhile from mine own company.
    (Lies down and sleeps.)

PUCK. Yet but three? Come one more;
Two of both kinds makes up four.
Here she comes, curst and sad:

₄₄₀ Cupid is a knavish lad,
Thus to make poor females mad.

(Re-enter HERMIA.)

HER. Never so weary, never so in woe;
Bedabbled with the dew, and torn with briers;
I can no further crawl, no further go;
₄₄₅ My legs can keep no pace with my desires.
Here will I rest me till the break of day.
Heavens shield Lysander, if they mean a fray!
(Lies down and sleeps.)
PUCK.
On the ground
Sleep sound:
₄₅₀ I'll apply
To your eye,
Gentle lover, remedy. *(Squeezing the juice on
Lysander's eyes.)*
When thou wakest,
Thou takest
₄₅₅ True delight
In the sight
Of thy former lady's eye:
And the country proverb known,
That every man should take his own,
₄₆₀ In your waking shall be shown:
Jack shall have Jill;
Nought shall go ill;
The man shall have his mare again, and all
shall be well. *(Exit.)*

ACT IV

SCENE I. *THE SAME.* LYSANDER, DEMETRIUS, HELENA, *AND* HERMIA *LYING ASLEEP.*

(ENTER TITANIA AND BOTTOM; PEASEBLOSSOM, COBWEB, MOTH, MUSTARDSEED, AND OTHER FAIRIES ATTENDING; OBERON BEHIND UNSEEN.)

TITA. Come, sit thee down upon this flowery
    bed,
While I thy amiable cheeks do coy,
And stick musk-roses in thy sleek smooth
    head,
And kiss thy fair large ears, my gentle joy.
005 **BOT.** Where's Peaseblossom?
PEAS. Ready.
BOT. Scratch my head, Peaseblossom.
    Where's Mounsieur Cobweb?
COB. Ready.

010 ***Bot.*** Mounsieur Cobweb, good
mounsieur, get you your weapons in your
hand, and kill me a red-hipped humble-
bee on the top of a thistle; and, good
mounsieur, bring me the honey-bag. Do
not fret yourself too much in the action,
mounsieur; and, good mounsieur, have a
care the honey-bag 015 break not; I would
be loth to have you overflown with a
honey-bag, signior. Where's Mounsieur
Mustardseed.

Mus. Ready.

Bot. Give me your neaf, Mounsieur
Mustardseed. Pray you, leave your
courtesy, good mounsieur.

020 ***Mus.*** What's your will?

Bot. Nothing, good mounsieur, but to help
Cavalery Cobweb to scratch. I must to the
barber's, mounsieur; for methinks I am
marvellous hairy about the face; and I am
such a tender ass, if my hair do but tickle
me, I must scratch.

025 ***Tita.*** What, wilt thou hear some music,
my sweet love?

Bot. I have a reasonable good ear in music.
Let's have the tongs and the bones.

Tita. Or say, sweet love, what thou desirest
to eat.

Bot. Truly, a peck of provender: I could
munch your 030 good dry oats. Methinks I

have a great desire to a bottle of hay:
good hay, sweet hay, hath no fellow.

TITA. I have a venturous fairy that shall seek
The squirrel's hoard, and fetch thee new nuts.

BOT. I had rather have a handful or two of
dried peas. 035 But, I pray you, let none of
your people stir me: I have an exposition
of sleep come upon me.

TITA. Sleep thou, and I will wind thee in my
arms.
Fairies, be gone, and be all ways away. *(Exeunt
Fairies.)*
So doth the woodbine the sweet honeysuckle
040 Gently entwist; the female ivy so
Enrings the barky fingers of the elm.
O, how I love thee! how I dote on thee! *(They
sleep.)*

(Enter PUCK.)

OBE. *(Advancing)* Welcome, good Robin.
See'st thou this sweet sight?
Her dotage now I do begin to pity:
045 For, meeting her of late behind the wood,
Seeking sweet favours for this hateful fool,
I did upbraid her, and fall out with her;
For she his hairy temples then had rounded
With coronet of fresh and fragrant flowers;
050 And that same dew, which sometime on
the buds

73

Was wont to swell, like round and orient
    pearls,
Stood now within the pretty flowerets' eyes,
Like tears, that did their own disgrace bewail.
When I had at my pleasure taunted her,
₀₅₅ And she in mild terms begg'd my patience,
I then did ask of her her changeling child;
Which straight she gave me, and her
    fairy sent
To bear him to my bower in fairy land.
And now I have the boy, I will undo
₀₆₀ This hateful imperfection of her eyes:
And, gentle Puck, take this transformed scalp
From off the head of this Athenian swain;
That, he awaking when the other do,
May all to Athens back again repair,
₀₆₅ And think no more of this night's
    accidents,
But as the fierce vexation of a dream.
But first I will release the fairy queen.
Be as thou wast wont to be;
See as thou wast wont to see:
₀₇₀ Dian's bud o'er Cupid's flower
Hath such force and blessed power.
Now, my Titania; wake you, my sweet queen.
TITA. My Oberon! what visions have I seen!
Methought I was enamour'd of an ass.
OBE. There lies your love.
TITA.
₀₇₅ How came these things to pass?
O, how mine eyes do loathe his visage now!

OBE. Silence awhile. Robin, take off this
    head.
Titania, music call; and strike more dead
Than common sleep of all these five the
    sense.
080 **TITA.** Music, ho! music, such as charmeth
    sleep! *(Music, still.)*
PUCK. Now, when thou wakest, with thine
    own fool's eyes peep.
OBE. Sound, music! Come, my queen, take
    hands with me,
And rock the ground whereon these sleepers
    be.
Now thou and I are new in amity,
085 And will to-morrow midnight solemnly
Dance in Duke Theseus' house triumphantly,
And bless it to all fair prosperity:
There shall the pairs of faithful lovers be
Wedded, with Theseus, all in jollity.
PUCK.
090 Fairy king, attend, and mark:
I do hear the morning lark.
OBE.
Then, my queen, in silence sad,
Trip we after the night's shade:
We the globe can compass soon,
095 Swifter than the wandering moon.
TITA.
Come, my lord; and in our flight,
Tell me how it came this night,
That I sleeping here was found

With these mortals on the ground. *(Horns
winded within.) (Exeunt.)*

(ENTER THESEUS, HIPPOLYTA, EGEUS, AND TRAIN.)

₁₀₀ *THE.* Go, one of you, find out the forester;
For now our observation is perform'd;
And since we have the vaward of the day,
My love shall hear the music of my hounds.
Uncouple in the western valley; let them go:
₁₀₅ Dispatch, I say, and find the forester. *(Exit
an Attend.)*
We will, fair queen, up to the mountain's top,
And mark the musical confusion
Of hounds and echo in conjunction.
HIP. I was with Hercules and Cadmus once,
₁₁₀ When in a wood of Crete they bay'd
the bear
With hounds of Sparta: never did I hear
Such gallant chiding; for, besides the groves,
The skies, the fountains, every region near
Seem'd all one mutual cry: I never heard
₁₁₅ So musical a discord, such sweet thunder.
THE. My hounds are bred out of the Spartan
kind,
So flew'd, so sanded; and their heads
are hung
With ears that sweep away the morning
dew;
Crook-knee'd, and dew-lapp'd like Thessalian
bulls;

₁₂₀ Slow in pursuit, but match'd in mouth like
  bells,
Each under each. A cry more tuneable
Was never holla'd to, nor cheer'd with horn,
In Crete, in Sparta, nor in Thessaly:
Judge when you hear. But, soft! what nymphs
  are these?

₁₂₅ *EGE.* My lord, this is my daughter here
  asleep;
And this, Lysander; this Demetrius is;
This Helena, old Nedar's Helena:
I wonder of their being here together.

THE. No doubt they rose up early to observe
₁₃₀ The rite of May; and, hearing our intent,
Came here in grace of our solemnity.
But speak, Egeus; is not this the day
That Hermia should give answer of her
  choice?

EGE. It is, my lord.

₁₃₅ *THE.* Go, bid the huntsmen wake them
  with their horns. *(Horns and shout within.)*
  (Lys., Dem., Hel., and Her., wake and start up.)
Good morrow, friends. Saint Valentine is past:
Begin these wood-birds but to couple now?

LYS. Pardon, my lord.

THE. I pray you all, stand up.
I know you two are rival enemies:
₁₄₀ How comes this gentle concord in the
  world,
That hatred is so far from jealousy,
To sleep by hate, and fear no enmity?

LYS. My lord, I shall reply amazedly,
Half sleep, half waking: but as yet, I swear,
145 I cannot truly say how I came here;
But, as I think,—for truly would I speak,
And now I do bethink me, so it is,—
I came with Hermia hither: our intent
Was to be gone from Athens, where we
    might,
150 Without the peril of the Athenian law.
EGE. Enough, enough, my lord; you have
    enough:
I beg the law, the law, upon his head.
They would have stolen away; they would,
    Demetrius,
Thereby to have defeated you and me,
155 You of your wife and me of my consent,
Of my consent that she should be your wife.
DEM. My lord, fair Helen told me of their
    stealth,
Of this their purpose hither to this wood;
And I in fury hither follow'd them,
160 Fair Helena in fancy following me.
But, my good lord, I wot not by what power,

—

But by some power it is,—my love to Hermia,
Melted as the snow, seems to me now
As the remembrance of an idle gaud,
165 Which in my childhood I did dote upon;
And all the faith, the virtue of my heart,
The object and the pleasure of mine eye,
Is only Helena. To her, my lord,

Was I betroth'd ere I saw Hermia:
₁₇₀ But, like in sickness, did I loathe this food;
But, as in health, come to my natural taste,
Now I do wish it, love it, long for it,
And will for evermore be true to it.

THE. Fair lovers, you are fortunately met:
₁₇₅ Of this discourse we more will hear anon.
Egeus, I will overbear your will;
For in the temple, by and by, with us
These couples shall eternally be knit:
And, for the morning now is something worn,
₁₈₀ Our purposed hunting shall be set aside.
Away with us to Athens! three and three,
We'll hold a feast in great solemnity.
Come, Hippolyta. *(Exeunt The., Hip., Ege., and
    train.)*

DEM. These things seem small and
    undistinguishable,
₁₈₅ Like far-off mountains turned into clouds.

HER. Methinks I see these things with
    parted eye,
When every thing seems double.

HEL. So methinks:
And I have found Demetrius like a jewel,
Mine own, and not mine own.

DEM.
Are you sure
₁₉₀ That we are awake? It seems to me
That yet we sleep, we dream. Do not you
    think
The Duke was here, and bid us follow him?

HER. Yea; and my father.

HEL. And Hippolyta.

LYS. And he did bid us follow to the temple.

195 **DEM.** Why, then, we are awake: let's follow him;

And by the way let us recount our dreams.
(Exeunt.)

BOT. *(Awaking)* When my cue comes, call me, and I will answer: my next is, 'Most fair Pyramus.' Heigh-ho! Peter Quince! Flute, the bellows-mender! Snout, the 200 tinker! Starveling! God's my life, stolen hence, and left me asleep! I have had a most rare vision. I have had a dream, past the wit of man to say what dream it was: man is but an ass, if he go about to expound this dream. Methought I was—there is no man can tell what. Methought I was,— and methought I had,—but man is but a patched 205 fool, if he will offer to say what methought I had. The eye of man hath not heard, the ear of man hath not seen, man's hand is not able to taste, his tongue to conceive, nor his heart to report, what my dream was. I will get Peter Quince 210 to write a ballad of this dream: it shall be called Bottom's Dream, because it hath no bottom; and I will sing it in the latter end of a play, before the Duke: peradventure, to make it the more gracious, I shall sing it at her death. *(Exit.)*

SCENE II. ATHENS. QUINCE'S HOUSE.

(Enter Quince, Flute, Snout, and Starveling.)

Quin. Have you sent to Bottom's house? is
he come home yet?

Star. He cannot be heard of. Out of doubt
he is transported.

005 **Flu.** If he come not, then the play is
marred: it goes not forward, doth it?

Quin. It is not possible: you have not a man
in all Athens able to discharge Pyramus
but he.

Flu. No, he hath simply the best wit of any
handicraft 010 man in Athens.

Quin. Yea, and the best person too; and he is
a very paramour for a sweet voice.

Flu. You must say 'paragon': a paramour is,
God bless us, a thing of naught.

(Enter Snug.)

015 **Snug.** Masters, the Duke is coming from
the temple, and there is two or three lords
and ladies more married: if our sport had
gone forward, we had all been made men.

Flu. O sweet bully Bottom! Thus hath he
lost sixpence a day during his life; he
could not have scaped sixpence 020 a day:
an the Duke had not given him sixpence a
day for playing Pyramus, I'll be hanged;

he would have deserved it: sixpence a day
in Pyramus, or nothing.

(Enter Bottom.)

Bot. Where are these lads? where are these
hearts?

Quin. Bottom! O most courageous day! O
most $_{025}$ happy hour!

Bot. Masters, I am to discourse wonders: but
ask me not what; for if I tell you, I am no
true Athenian. I will tell you every thing,
right as it fell out.

Quin. Let us hear, sweet Bottom.

$_{030}$ **Bot.** Not a word of me. All that I will tell
you is, that the Duke hath dined. Get your
apparel together, good strings to your
beards, new ribbons to your pumps; meet
presently at the palace; every man look
o'er his part; for the short and the long is,
our play is preferred. In any $_{035}$ case, let
Thisby have clean linen; and let not him
that plays the lion pare his nails, for they
shall hang out for the lion's claws. And,
most dear actors, eat no onions nor garlic,
for we are to utter sweet breath; and I do
not doubt but to hear them say, it is a
sweet comedy. No more $_{040}$ words: away!
go, away! *(Exeunt.)*

ACT V

SCENE I. ATHENS. THE PALACE OF
THESEUS.

*(Enter THESEUS, HIPPOLYTA, PHILOSTRATE, Lords, and
Attendants.)*

HIP. 'Tis strange, my Theseus, that these
    lovers speak of.
THE. More strange than true: I never may
    believe
These antique fables, nor these fairy toys.
Lovers and madmen have such seething
    brains,
005 Such shaping fantasies, that apprehend
More than cool reason ever comprehends.
The lunatic, the lover and the poet
Are of imagination all compact:
One sees more devils than vast hell can hold,
010 That is, the madman: the lover, all as
    frantic,
Sees Helen's beauty in a brow of Egypt:
The poet's eye, in a fine frenzy rolling,

Doth glance from heaven to earth, from earth
    to heaven;
And as imagination bodies forth
015 The forms of things unknown, the
    poet's pen
Turns them to shapes, and gives to airy
    nothing
A local habitation and a name.
Such tricks hath strong imagination,
That, if it would but apprehend some joy,
020 It comprehends some bringer of that joy;
Or in the night, imagining some fear,
How easy is a bush supposed a bear!
HIP. But all the story of the night told over,
And all their minds transfigured so together,
025 More witnesseth than fancy's images,
And grows to something of great constancy;
But, howsoever, strange and admirable.
THE. Here come the lovers, full of joy and
    mirth.

(ENTER LYSANDER, DEMETRIUS, HERMIA, AND
HELENA.)

Joy, gentle friends! joy and fresh days of love
Accompany your hearts!
LYS. 030 More than to us
Wait in your royal walks, your board, your bed!
THE. Come now; what masques, what dances
    shall we have,

To wear away this long age of three hours
Between our after-supper and bed-time?
₀₃₅ Where is our usual manager of mirth?
What revels are in hand? Is there no play,
To ease the anguish of a torturing hour?
Call Philostrate.

PHIL. Here, mighty Theseus.

THE. Say, what abridgement have you for this
    evening?
₀₄₀ What masque? what music? How shall we
    beguile
The lazy time, if not with some delight?

PHIL. There is a brief how many sports are
    ripe:
Make choice of which your highness will see
    first. *(Giving a paper.)*

THE. *(reads)* The battle with the Centaurs, to
    be sung
₀₄₅ By an Athenian eunuch to the harp.
We'll none of that: that have I told my love,
In glory of my kinsman Hercules.
(Reads) The riot of the tipsy Bacchanals,
Tearing the Thracian singer in their rage.
₀₅₀ That is an old device; and it was play'd
When I from Thebes came last a conqueror.
(Reads) The thrice three Muses mourning for
    the death
Of Learning, late deceased in beggary.
That is some satire, keen and critical,
₀₅₅ Not sorting with a nuptial ceremony.

85

(Reads) A tedious brief scene of young
    Pyramus
And his love Thisbe; very tragical mirth.
Merry and tragical! tedious and brief!
That is, hot ice and wondrous strange snow.
060 How shall we find the concord of this
    discord?
PHIL. A play there is, my lord, some ten
    words long,
Which is as brief as I have known a play;
But by ten words, my lord, it is too long,
Which makes it tedious; for in all the play
065 There is not one word apt, one player
    fitted:
And tragical, my noble lord, it is;
For Pyramus therein doth kill himself.
Which, when I saw rehearsed, I must confess,
Made mine eyes water; but more merry tears
070 The passion of loud laughter never shed.
THE. What are they that do play it?
PHIL. Hard-handed men, that work in
    Athens here,
Which never labour'd in their minds till now;
And now have toil'd their unbreathed
    memories
075 With this same play, against your nuptial.
THE. And we will hear it.
PHIL. No, my noble lord;
It is not for you: I have heard it over,
And it is nothing, nothing in the world;
Unless you can find sport in their intents,

080 Extremely stretch'd and conn'd with cruel
    pain,
To do you service.
THE. I will hear that play;
For never any thing can be amiss,
When simpleness and duty tender it.
Go, bring them in: and take your places,
    ladies. *(Exit Philostrate.)*
085 ***HIP.*** I love not to see wretchedness
    o'ercharged,
And duty in his service perishing.
THE. Why, gentle sweet, you shall see no such
    thing.
HIP. He says they can do nothing in this
    kind.
THE. The kinder we, to give them thanks for
    nothing.
090 Our sport shall be to take what they
    mistake:
And what poor duty cannot do, noble respect
Takes it in might, not merit.
Where I have come, great clerks have
    purposed
To greet me with premeditated welcomes;
095 Where I have seen them shiver and look
    pale,
Make periods in the midst of sentences,
Throttle their practised accent in their fears,
And, in conclusion, dumbly have broke off,
Not paying me a welcome. Trust me, sweet,
100 Out of this silence yet I pick'd a welcome;

And in the modesty of fearful duty
I read as much as from the rattling tongue
Of saucy and audacious eloquence.
Love, therefore, and tongue-tied simplicity
105 In least speak most, to my capacity.

(RE-ENTER PHILOSTRATE.)

PHIL. So please your Grace, the Prologue is
address'd.
THE. Let him approach. *(Flourish of trumpets.)*

(Enter QUINCE for the Prologue.)

PRO. If we offend, it is with our good will.
That you should think, we come not to
offend,
110 But with good will. To show our simple
skill,
That is the true beginning of our end.
Consider, then, we come but in despite.
We do not come as minding to content you,
Our true intent is. All for your delight,
115 We are not here. That you should here
repent you,
The actors are at hand; and, by their show,
You shall know all, that you are like to know.
THE. This fellow doth not stand upon
points.
LYS. He hath rid his prologue like a rough
colt; he knows not the stop. A good moral,

my lord: it is not $_{120}$ enough to speak, but
to speak true.

HIP. Indeed he hath played on his prologue
like a child on a recorder; a sound, but
not in government.

THE. His speech was like a tangled chain;
nothing impaired, $_{125}$ but all disordered.
Who is next?

*(ENTER PYRAMUS AND THISBE, WALL, MOONSHINE,
AND LION.)*

PRO. Gentles, perchance you wonder at this
show;

But wonder on, till truth make all things
plain.

This man is Pyramus, if you would know;

This beauteous lady Thisby is certain.

$_{130}$ This man, with lime and rough-cast, doth
present

Wall, that vile Wall which did these lovers
sunder;

And through Wall's chink, poor souls, they
are content

To whisper. At the which let no man wonder.

This man, with lanthorn, dog, and bush of
thorn,

$_{135}$ Presenteth Moonshine; for, if you will
know,

By moonshine did these lovers think no scorn
To meet at Ninus' tomb, there, there to woo.

This grisly beast, which Lion hight by name,
The trusty Thisby, coming first by night,
₁₄₀ Did scare away, or rather did affright;
And, as she fled, her mantle she did fall,
Which Lion vile with bloody mouth did stain.
Anon comes Pyramus, sweet youth and tall,
And finds his trusty Thisby's mantle slain:
₁₄₅ Whereat, with blade, with bloody blameful
blade,
He bravely broach'd his boiling bloody breast;
And Thisby, tarrying in mulberry shade,
His dagger drew, and died. For all the rest,
Let Lion, Moonshine, Wall, and lovers twain
₁₅₀ At large discourse, while here they do
remain. *(Exeunt Prologue, Thisbe, Lion, and
Moonshine.)*

THE. I wonder if the lion be to speak.
DEM. No wonder, my lord: one lion may,
when many
asses do.
WALL. In this same interlude it doth befall
₁₅₅ That I, one Snout by name, present a wall;
And such a wall, as I would have you think,
That had in it a crannied hole or chink,
Through which the lovers, Pyramus and
Thisby,
Did whisper often very secretly.
₁₆₀ This loam, this rough-cast, and this stone,
doth show
That I am that same wall; the truth is so:
And this the cranny is, right and sinister,

Through which the fearful lovers are to
    whisper.

THE. Would you desire lime and hair to
    speak better?

165 **DEM.** It is the wittiest partition that ever I
    heard discourse, my lord.

THE. Pyramus draws near the wall: silence!

(ENTER PYRAMUS.)

PYR. O grim-look'd night! O night with hue
    so black!

O night, which ever art when day is not!

170 O night, O night! alack, alack, alack,

I fear my Thisby's promise is forgot!

And them, O wall, O sweet, O lovely wall,

That stand'st between her father's ground
    and mine!

Thou wall, O wall, O sweet and lovely wall,

175 Show me thy chink, to blink through with
    mine eyne! *(Wall holds up his fingers.)*

Thanks, courteous wall: Jove shield thee well
    for this!

But what see I? No Thisby do I see.

O wicked wall, through whom I see no bliss!

Cursed be thy stones for thus deceiving me!

THE. The wall, methinks, being sensible,
    should curse 180 again.

PYR. No, in truth, sir, he should not.

    'Deceiving me' is Thisby's cue: she is to
    enter now, and I am to spy her through

the wall. You shall see, it will fall pat as I told ₁₈₅ you. Yonder she comes.

(ENTER THISBE.)

THIS. O wall, full often hast thou heard my moans,
For parting my fair Pyramus and me!
My cherry lips have often kiss'd thy stones,
Thy stones with lime and hair knit up in thee.
₁₉₀ **PYR.** I see a voice: now will I to the chink,
To spy an I can hear my Thisby's face.
Thisby!
THIS. My love thou art, my love I think.
PYR. Think what thou wilt, I am thy lover's grace;
₁₉₅ And, like Limander, am I trusty still.
THIS. And I like Helen, till the Fates me kill.
PYR. Not Shafalus to Procrus was so true.
THIS. As Shafalus to Procrus, I to you.
PYR. O, kiss me through the hole of this vile wall!
₂₀₀ **THIS.** I kiss the wall's hole, not your lips at all.
PYR. Wilt thou at Ninny's tomb meet me straightway?
THIS. 'Tide life, 'tide death, I come without delay. *(Exeunt Pyramus and Thisbe.)*
WALL. Thus have I, wall, my part discharged so;

And, being done, thus wall away doth go.
(Exit.)

205 **THE.** Now is the mural down between the two neighbours.

DEM. No remedy, my lord, when walls are so wilful to
hear without warning.

HIP. This is the silliest stuff that ever I heard.

210 **THE.** The best in this kind are but shadows; and the
worst are no worse, if imagination amend them.

HIP. It must be your imagination then, and not theirs.

THE. If we imagine no worse of them than they of
themselves, they may pass for excellent men. Here come

215 two noble beasts in a man and a lion.

(ENTER LION AND MOONSHINE.)

LION. You, ladies, you, whose gentle hearts do fear
The smallest monstrous mouse that creeps on floor,
May now perchance both quake and tremble here,
When lion rough in wildest rage doth roar.

220 Then know that I, one Snug the joiner, am
A lion-fell, nor else no lion's dam;

For, if I should as lion come in strife
Into this place, 'twere pity on my life.

THE. A very gentle beast, and of a good
conscience.

225 **DEM.** The very best at a beast, my lord,
that e'er I saw.

LYS. This lion is a very fox for his valour.

THE. True; and a goose for his discretion.

DEM. Not so, my lord; for his valour cannot
carry his discretion; and the fox carries
the goose.

230 **THE.** His discretion, I am sure, cannot
carry his valour; for the goose carries not
the fox. It is well: leave it to his discretion,
and let us listen to the moon.

MOON. This lanthorn doth the horned moon
present;—

DEM. He should have worn the horns on his
head.

235 **THE.** He is no crescent, and his horns are
invisible within the circumference.

MOON. This lanthorn doth the horned moon
present;
Myself the man i' the moon do seem to be.

THE. This is the greatest error of all the rest:
the man 240 should be put into the
lantern. How is it else the man i' the
moon?

DEM. He dares not come there for the
candle; for, you see, it is already in snuff.

HIP. I am aweary of this moon: would he
would $_{245}$ change!

THE. It appears, by his small light of
discretion, that he is in the wane; but yet,
in courtesy, in all reason, we must stay the
time.

LYS. Proceed, Moon.

$_{250}$ **MOON.** All that I have to say, is, to tell you
that the lanthorn is the moon; I, the man
in the moon; this thorn-bush, my thorn-
bush; and this dog, my dog.

DEM. Why, all these should be in the lantern;
for all these are in the moon. But, silence!
here comes Thisbe.

(ENTER THISBE.)

$_{255}$ **THIS.** This is old Ninny's tomb. Where is
my love?

LION. *(Roaring) Oh——— (Thisbe runs off.)*

DEM. Well roared, Lion.

THE. Well run, Thisbe.

HIP. Well shone, Moon. Truly, the moon
shines with $_{260}$ a good grace. *(The Lion
shakes Thisbe's mantle, and exit.)*

THE. Well moused, Lion.

DEM. And then came Pyramus.

LYS. And so the lion vanished.

(ENTER PYRAMUS.)

PYR. Sweet Moon, I thank thee for thy sunny
    beams;
265 I thank thee, Moon, for shining now so
    bright;
For, by thy gracious, golden, glittering gleams,
I trust to take of truest Thisby sight.
But stay, O spite!
But mark, poor knight,
270 What dreadful dole is here!
Eyes, do you see?
How can it be?
O dainty duck! O dear!
Thy mantle good,
275 What, stain'd with blood!
Approach, ye Furies fell!
O Fates, come, come,
Cut thread and thrum;
Quail, crush, conclude, and quell!
280 **THE.** This passion, and the death of a
    dear friend, would go near to make a man
    look sad.
HIP. Beshrew my heart, but I pity the man.
PYR. O wherefore, Nature, didst thou lions
    frame?
Since lion vile hath here deflower'd my dear:
285 Which is—no, no—which was the fairest
    dame
That lived, that loved, that liked, that look'd
    with cheer.
Come, tears, confound;
Out, sword, and wound

The pap of Pyramus;
290 Ay, that left pap,
Where heart doth hop: *(Stabs himself.)*
Thus die I, thus, thus, thus.
Now am I dead,
Now am I fled;
295 My soul is in the sky:
Tongue, lose thy light;
Moon, take thy flight: *(Exit Moonshine.)*
Now die, die, die, die, die. *(Dies.)*

DEM. No die, but an ace, for him; for he is
but one.

300 **LYS.** Less than an ace, man; for he is
dead; he is nothing.

THE. With the help of a surgeon he might yet
recover, and prove an ass.

HIP. How chance Moonshine is gone before
Thisbe 305 comes back and finds her
lover?

THE. She will find him by starlight. Here she
comes; and her passion ends the play.

(Re-enter THISBE.)

HIP. Methinks she should not use a long one
for such a Pyramus: I hope she will be
brief.

310 **DEM.** A mote will turn the balance, which
Pyramus, which Thisbe, is the better; he
for a man, God warrant us; she for a
woman, God bless us.

Lys. She hath spied him already with those
   sweet eyes.

Dem. And thus she means, videlicet:—

This. 315 Asleep, my love?

What, dead, my dove?

O Pyramus, arise!

Speak, speak. Quite dumb?

Dead, dead? A tomb

320 Must cover thy sweet eyes.

These lily lips,

This cherry nose,

These yellow cowslip cheeks,

Are gone, are gone:

325 Lovers, make moan:

His eyes were green as leeks.

O Sisters Three,

Come, come to me,

With hands as pale as milk;

330 Lay them in gore,

Since you have shore

With shears his thread of silk.

Tongue, not a word:

Come, trusty sword;

335 Come, blade, my breast imbrue: *(Stabs
   herself.)*

And, farewell, friends;

Thus Thisby ends:

Adieu, adieu, adieu. *(Dies.)*

The. Moonshine and Lion are left to bury
   the dead.

340 **Dem.** Ay, and Wall too.

BOT. *(Starting up)* No, I assure you; the wall is down that parted their fathers. Will it please you to see the epilogue, or to hear a Bergomask dance between two of our company?

345 **THE.** No epilogue, I pray you; for your play needs no excuse. Never excuse; for when the players are all dead, there need none to be blamed. Marry, if he that writ it had played Pyramus and hanged himself in Thisbe's garter, it would have been a fine tragedy: and so it is, truly; and 350 very notably discharged. But, come, your Bergomask: let your epilogue alone. *(A dance.)*

The iron tongue of midnight hath told twelve:

Lovers, to bed; 'tis almost fairy time.

I fear we shall out-sleep the coming morn,

355 As much as we this night have overwatch'd.

This palpable-gross play hath well beguiled

The heavy gait of night. Sweet friends, to bed.

A fortnight hold we this solemnity,

In nightly revels and new jollity. *(Exeunt.)*

(Enter PUCK.)

360 **PUCK.** Now the hungry lion roars,

And the wolf behowls the moon;

Whilst the heavy ploughman snores,
All with weary task fordone.
Now the wasted brands do glow,
365 Whilst the screech-owl, screeching loud,
Puts the wretch that lies in woe
In remembrance of a shroud.
Now it is the time of night,
That the graves, all gaping wide,
370 Every one lets forth his sprite,
In the church-way paths to glide:
And we fairies, that do run
By the triple Hecate's team,
From the presence of the sun,
375 Following darkness like a dream,
Now are frolic: not a mouse
Shall disturb this hallow'd house:
I am sent with broom before,
To sweep the dust behind the door.

(Enter OBERON and TITANIA with their train.)

380 **OBE.** Through the house give glimmering
    light,
By the dead and drowsy fire:
Every elf and fairy sprite
Hop as light as bird from brier;
And this ditty, after me,
385 Sing, and dance it trippingly.
TITA. First, rehearse your song by rote,
To each word a warbling note:
Hand in hand, with fairy grace,

Will we sing, and bless this place. *(Song and
  dance.)*
390 **OBE.** Now, until the break of day,
Through this house each fairy stray.
To the best bride-bed will we,
Which by us shall blessed be;
And the issue there create
395 Ever shall be fortunate.
So shall all the couples three
Ever true in loving be;
And the blots of Nature's hand
Shall not in their issue stand;
400 Never mole, hare lip, nor scar,
Nor mark prodigious, such as are
Despised in nativity,
Shall upon their children be.
With this field-dew consecrate,
405 Every fairy take his gait;
And each several chamber bless,
Through this palace, with sweet peace,
Ever shall in safety rest,
And the owner of it blest.
410 Trip away; make no stay;
Meet me all by break of day. *(Exeunt Oberon,
  Titania, and train.)*
PUCK. If we shadows have offended,
Think but this, and all is mended,
That you have but slumber'd here,
415 While these visions did appear.
And this weak and idle theme,
No more yielding but a dream,

Gentles, do not reprehend:
If you pardon, we will mend.
420 And, as I am an honest Puck,
If we have unearned luck
Now to scape the serpent's tongue,
We will make amends ere long;
Else the Puck a liar call:
425 So, good night unto you all.
Give me your hands, if we be friends,
And Robin shall restore amends. *(Exit.)*

Made in United States
North Haven, CT
28 April 2022

18679540R00071